Dowson First School

My Secret Pet

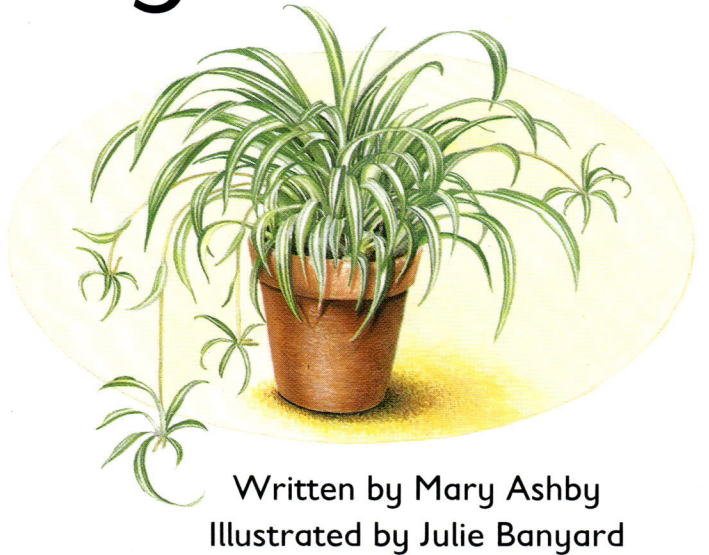

Written by Mary Ashby
Illustrated by Julie Banyard

Collins Educational

I have a pet.
But it's a secret.
No one knows but me.

My pet is very quiet.
Even my dad doesn't know about her.

My pet lives in a corner of my room.
She's no trouble.
I don't even need to feed her.

She gets her own food.
She catches her food in a sticky web.

The web is very thin. It stuck to my finger when I touched it. A piece came off, but she didn't seem to mind.

I gave her a dead fly once, but she wouldn't eat it. She just left it there.

One day I saw my pet catch a tiny fly. It nearly got away. But she threw some silk over it and it stopped moving.

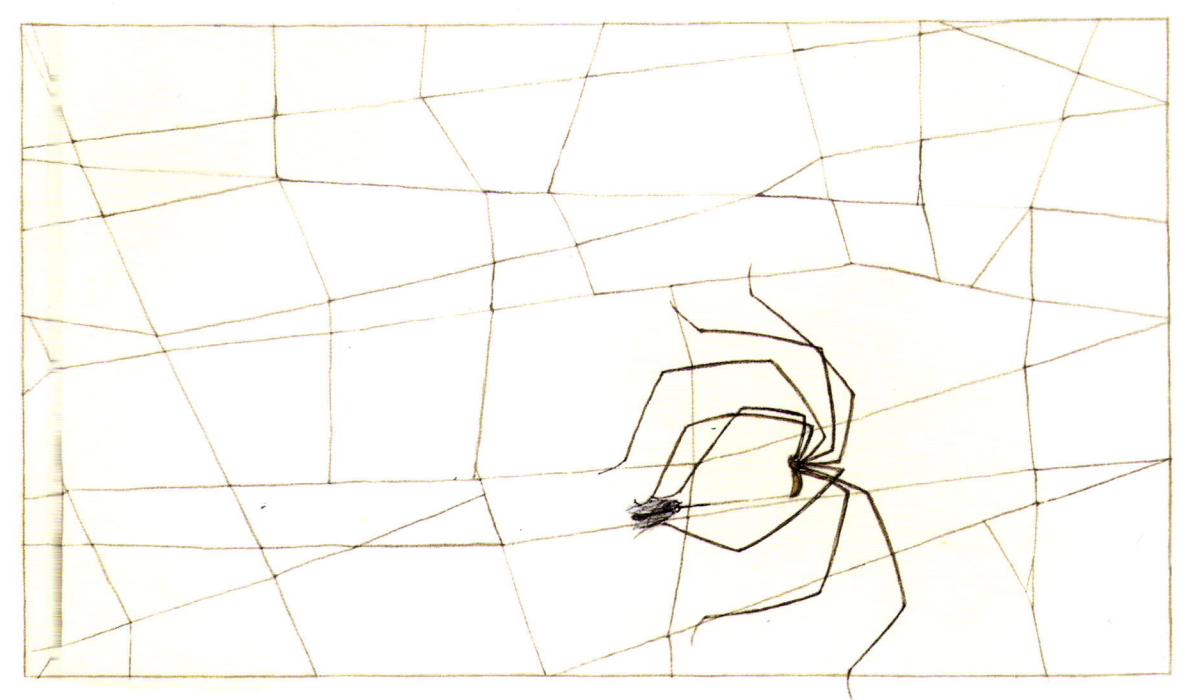

Then she wrapped it and wrapped it and wrapped it with new silk until it was all tied up.

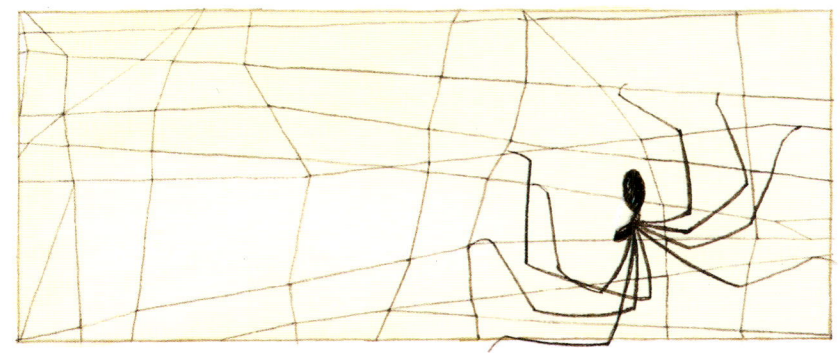

Then she gave it a bite. When I went to bed she was still holding it in her mouth. The next day it was gone.

I gave my pet a plant for company.
It was a spider plant. I think she liked it.

One day when I watered the plant, she came and got a drink.

After a while my pet's web began to get dusty and dirty. It didn't look very nice. And it wasn't very good for catching flies.

Then my dad saw it. He wasn't happy.
He got a broom and swept my pet's home away.
I thought my pet was gone forever.

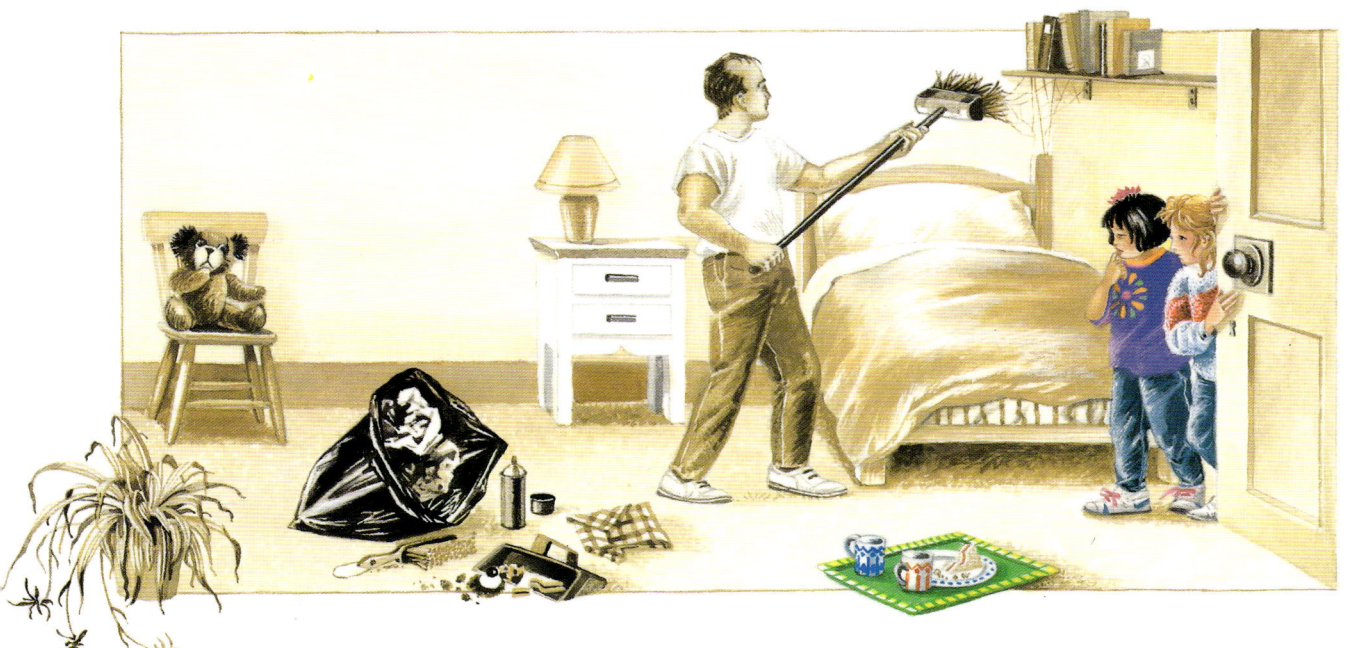

But the next day she was back.
She had made a new home for herself
when I was asleep. It was very clean.

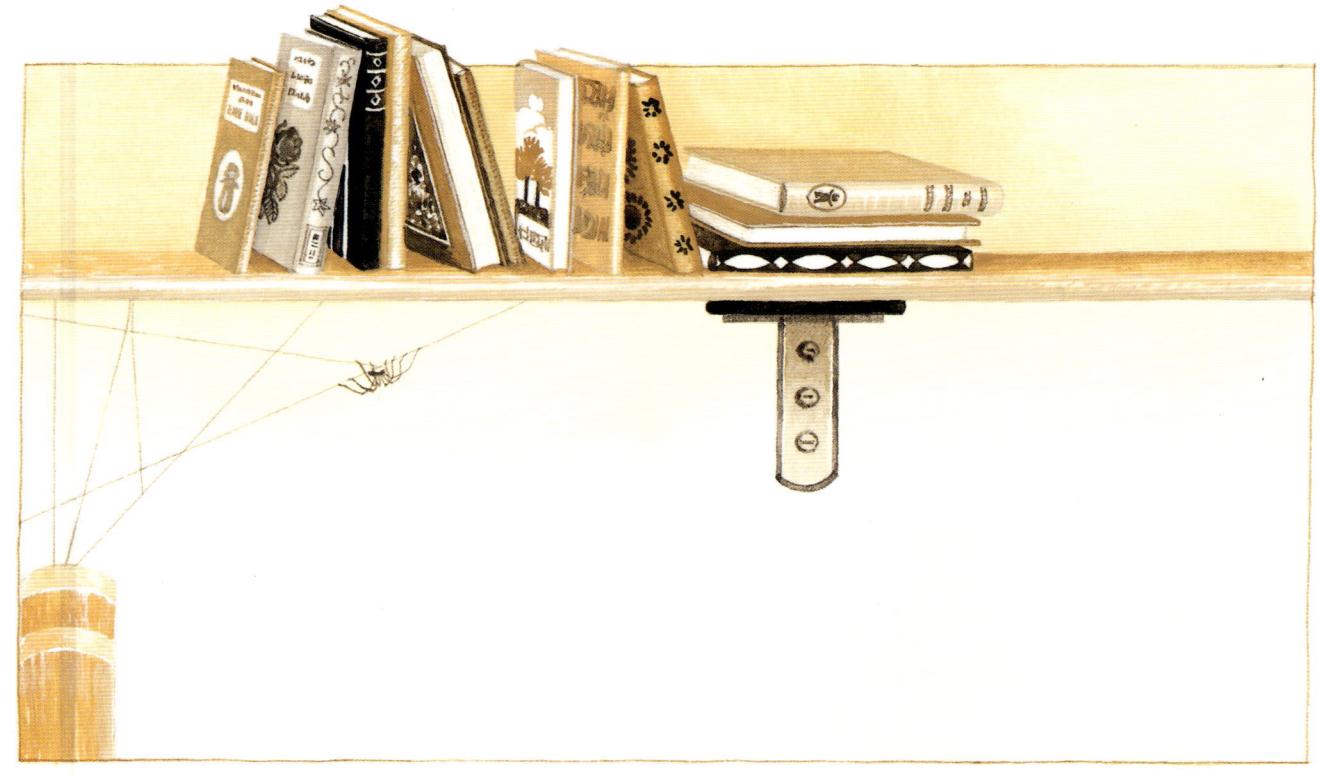

My dad didn't see it. But I did.

Spider facts

Spiders live in every part of the world: in houses, in gardens, in deserts, in jungles, in the Arctic, at the tops of mountains, under the ground and even under water.

There are over 600 different kinds of spiders in Great Britain, and over 30,000 in the world.

The spider in this story is called a *pholcus*. It always lives in houses, never outdoors. It is sometimes called a 'daddy-long-legs spider' because of its very long legs.

Spiders are helpful to people because they eat flies and other insect pests. Many people like spiders and enjoy watching them at work. Do you like watching spiders?